Original title:
Habit Liberation

Copyright © 2024 Creative Arts Management OÜ
All rights reserved.

Author: Thor Castlebury
ISBN HARDBACK: 978-9916-88-406-5
ISBN PAPERBACK: 978-9916-88-407-2

Unruly Adventures Await

The winds are calling out my name,
With whispers of a wild, untamed game.
Through forests thick and valleys wide,
I'll find the courage deep inside.

With each step taken, fears dissolve,
As mysteries around me evolve.
The uncharted paths cannot confine,
For every twist will be divine.

The Excitement of Unseen Pathways

Beneath the stars, the night ignites,
Tracks unseen lead to new heights.
Curiosity fuels my restless soul,
In shadows where hidden wonders unfold.

With every turn, a thrill unfolds,
New stories waiting to be told.
I chase the dawn, embracing the quest,
In unseen realms, I find my zest.

Journeys into the Wild Unknown

Through mountains high and rivers deep,
In nature's cradle, secrets keep.
The wild unknown beckons me near,
With every heartbeat, I shed my fear.

Footprints mark the paths I've roamed,
With each adventure, my spirit's honed.
In wild terrains, I learn to grow,
As life unfolds in vibrant flow.

The Chaotic Symphony of Change

Life's a dance of ebb and flow,
Where chaos reigns and colors glow.
In tangled beats, I find my song,
Embracing change, I journey along.

Each note a dare, each twist a chance,
In uncertainty, I choose to dance.
With joy and chaos intertwined,
A symphony of life, unconfined.

Dreams Set to Roam

In fields of stars where wishes float,
Soft whispers of the night we wrote.
With every step our hearts ignite,
A symphony of dreams takes flight.

The moonlight guides our timid feet,
As shadows dance, our fears retreat.
With open eyes, we chase the gleam,
Together we weave the thread of dream.

The Call of Uncharted Journeys

Beyond the hills, where wild winds sing,
Adventure waits with whispered wing.
Each path unknown, a promise bold,
To find the stories yet untold.

With hearts aglow, we heed the call,
To wander far, to leap, to fall.
In every turn, a chance to learn,
With every step, our spirits burn.

Lifting the Veil of Routine

Through the fog of daily grind,
A flicker of freedom we must find.
Breaking chains that hold us tight,
To see the world in a new light.

With every dawn that paints the sky,
We shake the dust of days gone by.
Renewed in spirit, bold and free,
Embracing life's sweet mystery.

Casting Off the Old Mask

In shadows deep, old fears remain,
But courage rises, breaks the chain.
With every tear, a truth we shed,
To find the self that lay ahead.

The mask we wore, once fit so tight,
Is cast aside, stepped into light.
Embracing flaws, we find our grace,
In every scar, a rightful place.

Embracing the Sweet Unknown

In the shadows, whispers call,
Adventures waiting, one and all.
With open hearts, we step in place,
Journey begins, a timeless chase.

Stars above, a guiding light,
Through the darkness, dreams take flight.
Every step, a tale unfolds,
In the unknown, the spirit bold.

The Breath of Unconventional Living

Paths untraveled, roads unmade,
In the chaos, we won't fade.
With wild hearts, we break the mold,
In every story, new and old.

Colors vibrant, shades unseen,
In the messy, find the clean.
Life's a canvas, paint your way,
Embrace the wild, seize the day.

Soaring Above the Mundane

Wings unfurled in morning light,
Breaking free from daily plight.
With every heartbeat, feeling high,
Above the clouds, we touch the sky.

Routine fades like morning dew,
In freedom's dance, we find what's true.
Each heartbeat leads to endless dreams,
Unshackled souls, or so it seems.

Embracing Change with Open Arms

Tides of life, they ebb and flow,
In the shifting winds, we grow.
With open hearts, we face the storm,
In every challenge, we transform.

Seasons change, yet beauty stays,
In the journey, find new ways.
With courage bright, we'll pave the path,
In every moment, feel the laugh.

Roads Less Traveled

In the woods where shadows play,
Silent paths lead far away.
Footprints linger, stories veiled,
Journey starts where few have sailed.

Rustling leaves, a whispered song,
Find the place where you belong.
Follow stars that light the way,
On the road where dreams can sway.

Each choice made, a step untold,
Hearts ignite, courage bold.
Winding trails, both rough and smooth,
In the wild, our spirits soothe.

The Symphony of New Beginnings

Beneath the dawn, a fresh refrain,
Hope awakens, breaks the chain.
Life's melody, soft and bright,
Plays with colors of the light.

Notes of laughter fill the air,
Echoes live beyond despair.
From the ashes, rise anew,
Striking chords, a vibrant hue.

Every heartbeat, every sigh,
Composes moments, flying high.
In this symphony we find,
A tapestry of dreams entwined.

Shattering Familiar Frames

Walls that box us, fade away,
Breaking molds, we dare to play.
Visions blurred become so clear,
Beyond the edge, there's nothing to fear.

In the chaos, art is born,
New horizons greet the dawn.
Fractured pieces fall like rain,
Whispers dance through joy and pain.

Unconventional routes unfold,
Stories vibrant, brave, and bold.
Free our minds, let loose the chains,
Shatter all familiar frames.

The Lure of Fresh Perspectives

Gaze beyond the common view,
Colors shift, the world feels new.
Each glance offers a chance to see,
Life unfolds in mystery.

Through the lens of chance and fate,
Open doors, don't hesitate.
In the blend of light and shade,
New discoveries are made.

Curiosity lights the spark,
Guiding us through realms of dark.
Change your stance, embrace the shift,
In fresh perspectives, find your gift.

Shifting Shadows of the Same Path

In the twilight's gentle breath,
Whispers of dreams softly tread,
Footsteps echo on the ground,
Yet in silence, truths abound.

Shadows dance in fleeting light,
Memories linger out of sight,
Every turn a choice to make,
Journey shared, yet hearts awake.

Paths may twist and diverge wide,
But the soul's truth cannot hide,
With every shadow, a new chance,
To embrace life's daring dance.

Under stars, the night will gleam,
Shifting shadows weave a dream,
Together we can find our way,
In the dawn of a brand new day.

The Canvas of Spontaneous Colors

Brushstrokes fluid, wild and free,
Colors blend in harmony,
Every hue a whispered song,
Artful chaos where we belong.

On the canvas possibilities,
Sparkling with vibrant mysteries,
Imagination paints the scene,
Creating worlds yet unseen.

Splashes of joy, drips of pain,
Mixing laughter with the rain,
Each stroke tells a different tale,
Life's delight can never pale.

In this art, we find our voice,
In every shade, a deeper choice,
The canvas calls, we hear its plea,
To embrace our wild artistry.

The Unfurling of Life's Possibilities

Petals open to greet the sun,
Each unfolding, a journey begun,
With every breath, horizons wide,
In life's garden, dreams reside.

Seasons change, and so do we,
Growth emerges, vibrant and free,
Opportunities in twilight glow,
In the nest of the mind, they grow.

Curiosity, a guiding star,
Inviting us to explore afar,
With open hearts, we chase the light,
Navigating through day and night.

With each step, new paths emerge,
In the dance of life, we surge,
The unfurling whispers secrets true,
Embracing all, the old and new.

Navigating Through Daring Waters

Waves crash with a timeless roar,
Each current challenges the shore,
In this sea, we learn to sail,
Finding courage in the gale.

Beneath the sky, vast and wide,
We seek the truth, uncurled, untied,
Charts may drift, but hearts stay strong,
In the deep, we all belong.

With every storm, we rise anew,
Strengthened by what we have been through,
Navigating through rough and calm,
In the waters, we find our balm.

Together we can brave the tides,
With hope's light as our guide,
Through daring waters, we will glide,
In life's voyage, side by side.

Wings of Unfamiliar Flight

Beneath the twilight sky we soar,
Where hopes unspoken long to explore.
A breeze ignites the heart's delight,
In shadows cast by dreams of flight.

A compass points to lands unknown,
With every step, the courage grown.
In feathers soft, we weave our fate,
To dance with stars and challenge fate.

Awakening from the Ordinary

In morning's sigh, the world awakes,
As sunlight spills, the silence breaks.
From weary eyes, new visions bloom,
Transforming life, dispelling gloom.

A whisper stirs the aging leaves,
And calls to hearts that yearn and grieve.
With every breath, we find the spark,
To chase the light beyond the dark.

The Freedom of Discarded Patterns

Chains that bind lose strength with time,
As rhythms shift, we seek to climb.
The fabric frays, but threads remain,
And in the change, we break the chain.

Once bound by labels, now we rise,
With painted wings that touch the skies.
In chaos found, a dance so free,
The heart's true song, our legacy.

Unshackled Dreams

With every heartbeat, visions grow,
From restless nights, our spirits flow.
A sky unveiled, we take our stance,
In moonlit paths, we find our chance.

Unchained from doubt, we learn to glide,
In whispers soft, our souls abide.
To paint the night with colors bright,
Unlocking dreams in vivid light.

Breaking Chains of Routine

In the morning light we rise,
Shadows of comfort in disguise.
Breaking free from yesterday's hold,
Embracing the new, brave and bold.

Each tick of the clock, a chance to grow,
Endless paths, waiting to show.
Whispers of change call from afar,
Guiding us like a distant star.

With every step, the chains fall away,
A dance with life, come what may.
Echoes of doubt fade in the sun,
Together we thrive, our journey begun.

Wings of Change

Soaring high on dreams untold,
With every heartbeat, we unfold.
The weight of fear, we cast aside,
As we follow the winds that guide.

Colors blend in the evening sky,
Painting visions of how to fly.
Embracing the moments, wild and free,
Unlocking the chains, just you and me.

In every flutter, a story spins,
In the rhythm of life, new hope begins.
We spread our wings, bold and bright,
Journeying forth into the night.

The Art of Letting Go

In the silence, we find our peace,
Releasing the worries that never cease.
Like leaves in autumn, we gently fall,
Embracing the freedom, answering the call.

Each breath a whisper, a soft goodbye,
To the burdens that weigh us down, oh my.
With open hearts, we make space anew,
For dreams to emerge and for skies to turn blue.

Moments once cherished, now fade away,
In the tapestry of life, come what may.
We learn the beauty in saying 'farewell',
The sweet satisfaction in breaking the shell.

Sunrise Over Old Patterns

At dawn, the sky begins to glow,
Casting light on paths we know.
Old patterns fade, like mist in the air,
As hope arises, vibrant and rare.

Golden hues break through the dark,
Igniting dreams, sparking a spark.
We shed the skin of who we were,
Embracing the dawn, hearts a-whir.

Each sunrise whispers of chances anew,
The beauty of change in every hue.
With courage, we step into the light,
Bidding farewell to the shadows of night.

Blossoms in Uncharted Soil

In the quiet of the morning light,
Seeds of hope break free from night.
With gentle care, they stretch and rise,
Beneath the vast, unclaimed skies.

Soft whispers drift on the breeze,
Telling tales of ancient trees.
Roots entwined in earth's embrace,
Life unfolds at its own pace.

Colors dance in wild array,
Petals bright, a bold display.
Nature's art, both fresh and new,
Blossoms bloom where dreams break through.

Stripping the Routine Away

Each tick of the clock, a silent plea,
Yearning for change, to set us free.
Routine wraps tight, a heavy chain,
We seek a path that breaks the strain.

With every step, we choose to roam,
Chasing the spark that feels like home.
Unraveling threads of the mundane,
Freedom whispers, let go the pain.

New horizons call our name,
In the shifts, we find the flame.
Stripping away what holds us tight,
Embracing the unknown, true delight.

The Colors of a Fresh Canvas

Splatters of paint, wild and free,
A canvas waits for what will be.
Brush in hand, a heart aglow,
Every stroke begins to flow.

Vivid hues and playful shades,
Dreams emerge as doubt now fades.
Layer by layer, visions form,
In creativity, we find the warm.

The boldest reds, the calmest blues,
Expressions born from love and muse.
On this canvas, life takes flight,
A masterpiece in morning light.

Beyond the Shadows of Yesterday

Echoes linger, shadows cast,
Holding stories from the past.
Yet beyond the dim and gray,
New chapters yearn to find their way.

With each dawn, the sun will rise,
Chasing away the darkest sighs.
Hope ignites, a spark so bright,
Guiding souls into the light.

We step forward, hearts ablaze,
Leaving behind the heavy haze.
Beyond the pain, we dare to dream,
Life unfolds like a flowing stream.

The Art of Unraveled Norms

In shadows where the whispers play,
We stitch the threads of a new day.
Conventions fray, the colors blend,
A dance begins, the rules we bend.

The canvas wide, our voices rise,
Breaking chains, we touch the skies.
With brush in hand, we paint the truth,
In strokes of courage, reclaiming youth.

Secrets linger in the air,
Bold reflections, beauty rare.
Each contour tells a tale untold,
A tapestry of brave and bold.

Within the chaos, find the grace,
In every step, reclaim space.
From norm to art, we forge the flame,
In the unknowing, we find our name.

Moments of Unsaid Yes

A glance across the crowded room,
A heart ignites beneath the gloom.
In silence, possibilities bloom,
With every breath, we sense the tune.

The pauses linger, time does freeze,
In hesitation, we find our keys.
A whisper soft, a breathy sigh,
In unspoken truth, we learn to fly.

The weight of wonder fills the air,
In every heartbeat, dreams laid bare.
With courage hidden in our hearts,
These moments wait, new life imparts.

So let us cherish all that's felt,
In quietude, the spark is dealt.
The unsaid yes, a promise clear,
In every glance, the world draws near.

Beyond the Comfort Cocoon

Nestled snug, where shadows cling,
The world outside begins to sing.
With every rustle, a call to roam,
Beyond the safe, we seek our home.

The wings unfurl, the tremors shake,
In fear's embrace, we dare to break.
Through echoes loud and whispers meek,
A journey starts, a future speaks.

With every step, the light will beam,
A place of hope, a vibrant dream.
The soft cocoon begins to yield,
To vast horizons, life's revealed.

In solitude, we find our strength,
Through trials faced, we grow in length.
Beyond the comfort, spirits soar,
In freedom's dance, we learn to roar.

Tides of Change Rush In

The waves crescendo, breaking fast,
In surges bold, the die is cast.
A tempest swells, the shore responds,
As change approaches, fate absconds.

With whispered secrets in the foam,
Each ebb and flow, a tale to roam.
The currents pull, relentless, wise,
In flowing tides, our spirits rise.

What once was firm, now shifts beneath,
In winds of change, we find our breath.
Through storms we sail, we navigate,
In courage found, we celebrate.

So let the tides reshape our path,
In waters deep, escape the wrath.
With open hearts, we dive right in,
To find the strength that lies within.

The Crescendo of Novel Choices

With every step we take anew,
The roads ahead are wide and true.
A symphony of paths untold,
In every choice, a dream unfolds.

The whispers call from distant lands,
To take the leap, to dare, to stand.
A melody of hopes arise,
In vibrant hues, the future lies.

As echoes form of what could be,
We dance along, wild and free.
In every heart, a spark ignites,
To shape our world with endless sights.

In the crescendo, find your way,
With each decision, seize the day.
For what we choose defines our tale,
In novel choices, dreams prevail.

Threads of Unwritten Stories

In silence weave the threads of time,
With every stitch, a tale to climb.
The gentle hands of fate unspool,
As stories wait, a sacred jewel.

In corners dim, the whispers grow,
Of lives unfurling, ebb and flow.
Each thread a life, a journey spun,
In every heart, the heat of sun.

Yet still unwritten, pages bare,
With ink of hope, the world will share.
So take your pen, let thoughts take flight,
And craft the stories born of light.

For every moment, every glance,
A thread connects within the dance.
Embrace the tales yet left to tell,
In unwritten stories, all is well.

Beyond the Wall of Comfort

A sturdy wall of safe retreat,
Where silence lingers, moments meet.
But just beyond, the wild awaits,
A world alive with vivid fates.

To venture forth, to break the mold,
With courage fierce and passion bold.
For comfort's arms can hold too tight,
And dim the flame of inner light.

Beyond the wall, the risks may soar,
With every leap, there's so much more.
Embrace the change, let shadows flee,
For in the unknown, we learn to be.

So tear the veil, step into grace,
Life's beauty blooms in every space.
Beyond the wall, the heart can soar,
In daring lives, we learn to score.

Unlocking the Enchanted Doors

In quiet corners, keys await,
The locks that hold our hearts' true fate.
With gentle hands and hopeful gaze,
We seek the light through mystic haze.

Each door a chapter, yet to read,
Where dreams and wishes plant their seed.
Unlock the magic, let it flow,
Each turn a chance to find the glow.

With every creak, a story breathes,
As whispered tales dance through the leaves.
For in these halls of wood and lore,
A universe behind each door.

So gather strength, and bravely dare,
To turn the key, embrace the air.
For in unlocking, we explore,
The magic waits behind the door.

The Liberation of Self

In silence I find my wings,
Soaring high, where freedom sings.
Shedding masks I once wore tight,
Embracing truth, stepping into light.

The mirror reflects a brand new face,
In this journey, I find my place.
No longer bound by fear or doubt,
I am strong, I am fierce, I am out.

With open heart, I greet the dawn,
Unchained spirit, my soul reborn.
Each step forward, a new embrace,
I am alive, I find my grace.

Breaking the Chains of Routine

The clock ticks slow, a steady beat,
Life in cycles, never sweet.
I crave the spark, the crisp new air,
To shatter patterns, break the snare.

Each sunrise calls, a chance to roam,
Beyond the walls that feel like home.
I'll dance where courage holds the light,
And cast away the gray of night.

In spontaneity, I find my song,
Rhythms of life where I belong.
With every choice, I feel the thrill,
To break the chains, to bend, to will.

The Dance of Spirited Change

The winds of change begin to swell,
In every heart, there lies a spell.
Embrace the shift, release the past,
In this grand dance, we're free at last.

Twisting, turning, a vibrant flow,
Life's a stage where we can grow.
With every beat, we rise and fall,
Together, we answer the call.

In courage found, we take the leap,
Awakening dreams buried deep.
With every motion, we reshape fate,
In this dance, we navigate.

Echoes of Unraveled Paths

Worn and weathered, the road unfolds,
Stories of journeys, of truths retold.
Each step echoes through time and space,
Whispers of wisdom in every place.

Lost in the shadows, I once did tread,
Where doubts and fears filled my head.
Yet light has emerged from every crack,
Guiding my spirit, I won't look back.

Paths diverge, yet all intertwine,
Threads of fate create a design.
With every heartbeat, I find my way,
Echoes of life, brightening the gray.

The Lightness of Being Unbound

In the morning's gentle glow,
Wings unfurl with a silent grace.
A heart, free from all weight,
Dances lightly in open space.

Dreams weave through the azure sky,
Lessons learned in whispered time.
Each breath a soft, sweet sigh,
In the rhythm, we find our rhyme.

With every step on untamed ground,
We shed the chains of yesterday.
Boundless hope is what we've found,
In the lightness, we drift away.

Eager souls chase the dawn's embrace,
Together, we greet the new day.
In the lightness of being unbound,
We discover all that's meant to stay.

New Horizons Beckon

Beneath the stars, a promise glows,
Whispers of dreams yet to arise.
Through valleys deep, adventure flows,
Toward the vast and painted skies.

Each step reveals a hidden path,
Guided by the moon's soft light.
In open fields, joy's aftermath,
In the quiet heart of night.

With every gust, the winds conspire,
To lead us where our spirits soar.
An endless quest, a growing fire,
New horizons, forever more.

Embrace the call, set forth with glee,
For every journey holds a spark.
New horizons beckon, wild and free,
In the wonder, we leave our mark.

The Echoes of Untamed Spirals

In the forest deep, whispers float,
Untamed spirals twist and weave.
Nature sings, a distant note,
In echoes where we dare believe.

Soft rustles sway under the moon,
Patterns form, a sacred dance.
In the wild, we find our tune,
From every glance, there's a chance.

Colors burst with primal force,
Awakening the dormant soul.
Every turn reveals the course,
In the journey, we become whole.

The echoes call, wild and sincere,
In the labyrinth, we'll take flight.
Through spirals' dance, we shed our fear,
In unity, we find the light.

Cravings for New Landscapes

Across the sands, a tale unfolds,
Each grain a journey, each step a story.
With hearts alight, we seek the bold,
In craving winds, we find our glory.

Mountains rise, kissed by the sun,
Their peaks invite our weary feet.
Where rivers merge and currents run,
In their depths, our dreams repeat.

Desires stretch to distant shores,
Where the ocean meets the sky.
With every wave, adventure roars,
In horizons vast, we learn to fly.

Cravings lead to greener fields,
As the world opens, vast and wide.
In new landscapes, our spirit yields,
To the wonder, we now abide.

Embracing the Unfamiliar

In shadows deep, I find my way,
With every step, the fears decay.
A whisper soft, the heart will guide,
Into the night where dreams abide.

The paths unknown, a dance of grace,
I leave behind a familiar place.
In endless skies, I spread my wings,
Each moment new, the freedom brings.

Waves crash loud on shores unseen,
In foreign lands, my spirit's keen.
To face the chance, to taste the thrill,
In every doubt, I find the will.

With open arms, I greet the strange,
In every twist, I welcome change.
For in the dark, new light will bloom,
Embracing all, dispelling gloom.

Echoes of Freedom

Beneath the stars, the night is free,
Whispers of hope like a gentle sea.
The chains once held begin to break,
In the stillness, I hear the wake.

Voices rise like a bird in flight,
Calling out through the aching night.
In every heart, a fire ignites,
Echoes of dreams in soaring heights.

No longer bound by fear and doubt,
I chant the words of a hopeful shout.
In unity, we find our way,
As freedom's song begins to play.

With every breath, I claim my right,
To chase the dawn, to seek the light.
A journey vast, a life unchained,
In echoes sweet, my heart has gained.

The Dance of New Beginnings

In twilight's glow, a spark ignites,
With every dawn, the heart takes flight.
A dance unfolds, both sweet and bright,
Embracing change, the soul's delight.

The past behind, a gentle sway,
In rhythms bold, I'm led away.
Each step I take, I mend and grow,
In vibrant hues, my spirit glows.

Through trials faced, I learn to leap,
In every fall, new seeds I reap.
The tapestry of dreams expands,
With open heart, I make my plans.

With every turn, a chance to bloom,
In gardens rich, dispelling gloom.
The dance continues, forever bright,
As new beginnings light the night.

Shattering Glass Walls

In silent rooms where echoes dwell,
A fractured dream begins to swell.
With courage built on whispered fears,
I take a breath to dry the tears.

With hands of strength, I find the seams,
To break the walls that cage our dreams.
Each shard that falls reveals the truth,
In shimmering light, reclaimed my youth.

Through crystal pain, I learn to fight,
Bit by bit, I reclaim my right.
The world outside, so vast and bright,
A journey starts beyond the night.

With every crack, a vision clear,
The freedom calls, I have no fear.
In unity, we rise and stand,
Together strong, hand in hand.

The Thrill of the Unfamiliar

A path unwalked, the air feels new,
Whispers of chance, with each step, pursue.
Curiosity blooms, a wild refrain,
The heart races forth, liberated from pain.

New faces, strange places, colors so bright,
Every encounter ignites pure delight.
The world spins faster, horizons expand,
In the dance of the unknown, together we stand.

Adventure awaits in every nook,
Pages unwritten, in the heart, a book.
What happens next, no one can say,
In the thrill of the unfamiliar, we play.

Step by step, into the unknown,
Embracing the magic, we're never alone.
For life is a journey, wild and free,
In the thrill of the unfamiliar, we're truly we.

Dancing with Serendipity

In the quiet of fate, we twirl and spin,
Fortuitous moments whisper from within.
A chance encounter, laughter shared bright,
Together we dance, bathed in soft light.

The universe winks, a playful tease,
Guiding our steps, like a gentle breeze.
With every misstep, a new path we find,
Serendipity's touch, so tender, so kind.

Lost in the rhythm, we're light on our feet,
Every surprise brings a new heartbeat.
In this fleeting waltz, we're wild and free,
Dancing with serendipity, just you and me.

From dusk until dawn, we sway and glide,
In the magic of moments where dreams collide.
Cherishing chance, we savor the bliss,
In the dance of serendipity, our sweetest kiss.

The Freedom to Scatter Threads

A tapestry woven with whispers of fate,
Threads of our stories, connect and create.
Each strand a wonder, a fragment of time,
In the freedom to scatter, we find our rhyme.

With every connection, a new color blooms,
The fabric of life reveals hidden rooms.
Ties that we forge, each knot holds a dream,
In the freedom to scatter, we learn how to gleam.

Moments like silver, threads tangled and bright,
Navigating chaos, we embrace the light.
Our paths intertwine, through laughter and tears,
In the freedom to scatter, we conquer our fears.

Together we weave a rich, vibrant tale,
In the threads of existence, we never will fail.
For in every small choice, a world we can shape,
In the freedom to scatter, together we escape.

Flames of Unpredictable Motion

Flickers of fire dance, wild and free,
A whirlwind of passion, the essence of glee.
With every spark, we rise and descend,
Flames of unpredictable motion, we bend.

In the chaos of life, we find our spark,
Churning and whirling, embracing the dark.
Each twist and turn, a story to tell,
In the flames of unpredictability, we dwell.

Moments ignite like stars in the night,
Guided by dreams, chasing the light.
Together we weave through laughter and strife,
In the flames of motion, we kindle our life.

So let us burn bright, unfurling our wings,
Flying through life as the universe sings.
With hearts full of fire, we dance through the storm,
In the flames of unpredictable motion, we transform.

Serendipity's Gentle Pull

In the quiet of the dawn,
A soft breeze whispers low,
Paths converge unknowingly,
Where the wildflowers grow.

Chance encounters linger sweet,
Moments woven tight,
In the tapestry of fate,
Life unfolds in light.

Unseen hands will guide us,
Through twists both big and small,
Embracing every turn,
Hear the universe call.

With a heart that's open wide,
We'll dance upon the stray,
Serendipity will lead,
To joys along the way.

The Embrace of New Light

Morning breaks with tender grace,
Shadows softly fade away,
Colors stretch across the sky,
Welcoming the day.

Hope renews in warming beams,
As doubts begin to part,
The sun ignites the silent dreams,
That linger in the heart.

Each ray a gentle promise,
Of new things yet to see,
In the glow of morning's touch,
We find our liberty.

In the embrace of new light,
We learn to love the chance,
To step into the brightness,
And let our spirits dance.

Leaps into the Abundant Unknown

With every breath a chance to soar,
Into realms we've never known,
Casting aside the fears of yore,
In the courage that we've grown.

The horizon calls with open arms,
To ventures bold and bright,
Each leap a taste of hidden charms,
Beneath the starlit night.

Floating on the winds of chance,
Our dreams begin to blend,
In the dance of circumstance,
New beginnings never end.

Embrace the unknown journey well,
With hope as our true guide,
In the leaps, our stories swell,
With love on every ride.

The Boundless Journey Ahead

A path unfurls beneath our feet,
With echoes of the past,
Each step a heartbeat, strong and sweet,
The journey's wide and vast.

Mountains rise and valleys fall,
With lessons to be learned,
In every whisper, every call,
A fire in us burns.

Through forests deep and rivers wide,
Adventure beckons still,
With every turn, we learn to glide,
Our spirits guided by will.

So let's embark on what's ahead,
With dreams that break the night,
In the boundless journey led,
We find our greatest light.

Unfurling the Soul

In the quiet dawn, dreams arise,
Whispers of hope, under wide skies.
Petals unfurl, revealing their grace,
A journey begins, a sacred space.

Gentle winds carry their song,
Inviting the heart to where it belongs.
Layers of fear start to peel,
Softening edges, making us feel.

Each step forward melts away night,
Bringing forth shadows to warm light.
The soul's embrace, a tender guide,
Revealing the beauty we try to hide.

The Awakening of Stagnation

In the stillness, silence reigns,
Time stands still, bound by chains.
Awakening dreams, stitched with care,
Stagnation whispers, it's time to dare.

Cracks in the surface, no longer can hide,
Flowing like water from inside.
Rusty gears begin to turn,
With every stirring, passions burn.

Each moment counts, make it clear,
Embrace the chaos, shed the fear.
From frozen ground, new life will grow,
Awakening winds start to blow.

Threads of a New Tapestry

Woven colors, rich and bright,
A tapestry born from day and night.
Each thread a story, silent and grand,
United in purpose, together they stand.

Fingers dance on the loom of time,
Intertwining hopes in rhythm and rhyme.
Yesterday's shadows blend with tomorrow,
Creating patterns from joy and sorrow.

With every tug, the fabric grows strong,
Resilience echoes a beautiful song.
In every stitch, a tale unfolds,
Of courage and love, forever retold.

The Path Less Traveled

Footprints lead where few dare roam,
Into the wild, we find our home.
Through tangled woods and mountains high,
The path less traveled beckons to fly.

With every step, we shed our fears,
Gathering wisdom through laughter and tears.
Curves and bends that twist and weave,
Whispers of secrets the heart must believe.

In solitude found, treasures awake,
Moments of stillness, each choice we make.
The journey unfolds, a life to embrace,
On the path less traveled, we find our place.

Unspooling the Predictable

In the thread of time we weave,
Pulling strands of what we believe,
Patterns formed in shadowed light,
Fraying edges hint at flight.

Each choice made, a turn to take,
Paths unfold with every break,
Looping back to where we start,
Unspooling tales that follow heart.

The familiar now feels strange,
In the dance of constant change,
Revealing truths we dare to face,
In the tapestry of space.

Through chaos comes a subtle peace,
As we let the known release,
Embracing every twist and thread,
In the stories left unsaid.

The Breath of Change

Whispers in the autumn breeze,
Carrying the scent of trees,
Leaves that flutter, drift, and sway,
Marking time as seasons play.

In moments brief, new paths arise,
Open hearts and widened eyes,
Embrace the shift, the bold unknown,
In every breath, a seed is sown.

With each dawn a chance to grow,
Letting go of what we know,
Suspended in the fleeting air,
The past dissolves, we breathe, we dare.

The tides of life, they ebb and flow,
Guiding us where we must go,
In this dance of shifting fate,
The breath of change we celebrate.

Reclaiming Lost Horizons

Beyond the fog, the echoes call,
Whispers haunting, shadows fall,
Once clear skies, now veiled in grey,
Yet hope ignites the path we stray.

Through the haze of fleeting years,
We gather dreams amid our fears,
Scanning skies for the sun's embrace,
Reclaiming lost horizons' grace.

With every step we seek the light,
Unfurling wings to take our flight,
The boundaries drawn begin to fray,
In the dawn of a brand new day.

So let us rise, break every chain,
Rebel against the weight of pain,
Together, hands in hands we'll go,
To find the places we once know.

Dance with the Unknown

In shadow's grip, we find the beat,
A rhythm soft beneath our feet,
The pulse of night invites the thrill,
To dance with dreams, embrace the chill.

With every twirl, the compass spins,
Lost in motion, where time begins,
To lean into the dark's embrace,
Daring steps find their rightful place.

In laughter's echo, we let go,
Our hearts ablaze with fires aglow,
Together in this swirling fate,
We learn to trust and celebrate.

So take my hand, let's lose control,
In the unknown, we find our soul,
A dance of life in vivid hues,
Embracing all that we might choose.

Colors Beyond the Gray

In a world draped in haze,
A flicker of light starts to play.
Each hue whispers soft, sweet refrain,
Breaking through all of the pain.

Crimson blossoms on the ground,
Emerald leaves dance all around.
Azure skies, a calming hold,
Painting dreams, both bright and bold.

Golden rays set the heart ablaze,
Transforming shadows, lifting praise.
In every corner, life takes flight,
Colors shine out, banishing night.

So let hope's palette guide your way,
Through the tumult, come what may.
Together we find, in every day,
Life's brilliance, beyond the gray.

Treading on Unseen Paths

Footsteps soft on ancient trails,
Wanderers weave their secret tales.
Beneath the stars, the night unfolds,
While dreams are born, and fate beholds.

Each twist and turn, a story made,
In hidden groves where shadows played.
A whisper calls from somewhere near,
Guiding hearts to persevere.

The moonlight pools on silver streams,
And every sigh unravels dreams.
Through tangled woods and time-worn stones,
We find our way, though all alone.

So tread with grace, embrace the night,
For unseen paths lead to the light.
In every step, the world reveals,
The magic of all that it conceals.

Seeds of Spontaneity

In quiet corners, dreams take root,
Unscripted moments in pursuit.
With a flutter, an idea blooms,
Chasing whims that break the gloom.

Laughter dances on the breeze,
Carried softly through the trees.
As hearts ignite, they learn to trust,
In chance and change, we find our thrust.

Each spark of joy, a seed we sow,
Unraveled plans begin to grow.
In serendipity's embrace,
Life flourishes, finding space.

So take the leap, embrace the wild,
Let spontaneity be your child.
In every moment, life expands,
With seeds of joy in open hands.

Whispers of Wandering Souls

Beneath the stars, a tale unfolds,
Of wandering hearts and dreams of old.
Through silent nights, they seek the flame,
To find their place, to make their name.

Echoes dance on the evening air,
Carrying stories of those who care.
In every whisper, a journey starts,
Connecting souls and binding hearts.

The road may bend, the path may sway,
Yet hope remains in disarray.
For in each step, a truth is known,
Wandering souls are never alone.

So listen close to the gentle sound,
Of lives entwined, forever bound.
In every heartbeat, a tale is spun,
Whispers of souls, forever one.

Reclaiming the Sunrise

In the hush of dawn's gentle glow,
Hope unfolds like petals slow.
Whispers rise with the breaking light,
Embracing shadows, turning bright.

Yesterday's burdens fall away,
As new dreams beckon to the day.
The sky's palette paints my soul,
Where once were fragments, now I'm whole.

Birds sing sweetly, pure and clear,
In each note, I shed my fear.
With every breath, the past I redeem,
Seeking more than just a dream.

I reclaim what time has lost,
Finding power in each cost.
The sunrise calls, I heed the sound,
In its embrace, my heart is found.

The Taste of Risky Ventures

Courage served on a silver plate,
Riding waves of unknown fate.
With each step, my heart beats fast,
In the thrill, I find my cast.

Stirring doubts whisper and tease,
Yet adventure's sweet breeze brings ease.
With open hands, I hold the thrill,
Filling my cup, I drink my fill.

Maps uncharted guide my way,
To lands where dreams dance and play.
The taste of risk ignites my spark,
Lighting pathways through the dark.

Each stumble teaches, each fall reveals,
The strength within that time congeals.
In every challenge, I'd rather tread,
Than live in comfort, dreams left dead.

From Bound to Brave

Chains that held I now discard,
With each struggle, growing hard.
From timid whispers to roars I soar,
Embracing battles, I seek more.

The past may linger like shadows still,
Yet within me grows a fiery will.
Every heartbeat, a promise to break,
In the face of fear, I shall awake.

Scaling mountains of doubt and despair,
I find my strength in the open air.
Each sunrise brings a brand new stage,
A story rewritten, I turn the page.

From bound to brave, my journey spins,
Embracing the chaos, I learn to win.
In the tapestry of life, I weave,
With threads of courage, I believe.

Mornings Unplanned

Awakened by the sun's warm kiss,
A canvas waits for blissful twist.
With coffee brewed and dreams anew,
I greet the day, my spirit true.

Unexpected paths unfold with grace,
In chaos, I find my sacred space.
Whispers of chance paint my way,
Every moment, a gift to play.

Laughter mingles with birds in song,
In the dance of life, I feel I belong.
Every mishap a chance to grow,
In the unplanned, my heart's aglow.

Mornings unchained bring joy to find,
In the messiness, love's entwined.
With open arms, I embrace the day,
In this wild ride, I choose to play.

Unlocked Opportunities Await

Open doors and whispered dreams,
In every heart, a fire gleams.
Chances rise like morning light,
Embrace the new, take flight tonight.

Step beyond the shadows cast,
Leave behind the doubts of past.
Adventure calls, it's time to steer,
In every risk, there's nothing to fear.

With every moment ripe for choice,
Listen closely to your voice.
In unopened paths, the brave find grace,
Opportunities in every space.

So spread your wings, let courage swell,
In the unknown, there lies a spell.
For hidden treasures come in hues,
If you dare, you cannot lose.

A Palette of Unconventional Choices

Colors mix in wildest ways,
In each brushstroke, chaos plays.
Life's a canvas, vast and bright,
Find your truth, unleash your light.

When others choose the paths well-trod,
Dare to wander, defy the odds.
Each option glimmers, sparkling bold,
In uniqueness, stories unfold.

Twist and turn the vibrant shades,
In the spectrum, freedom trades.
What's mundane becomes a spark,
In vivid hues, you make your mark.

So wield your brush with fierce delight,
And paint your world with love and fight.
For in the mix of bold and strange,
Lies the power to create and change.

The Thrill of Being Unpredictable

Life's a dance on shifting ground,
In spontaneity, joy is found.
Throw the rules out with the tide,
In surprises, let your heart reside.

Embrace the wild, the untried ways,
Live each moment, savor the days.
For constants fade like morning dew,
In the unknown, life feels anew.

Each twist and turn brings a thrill,
Moments captured, time to fill.
Be the spark that ignites the night,
With unpredictability, take flight.

In laughter shared and dreams unfurling,
Hold tight to the magic swirling.
For in the dance of chance today,
Find the beauty in the fray.

Paths Diverging in the Night

Two roads stretch in moonlit glow,
Winding softly where few dare go.
Whispers echo from the trees,
Each step forward stirs the breeze.

Choices linger in the cool air,
Heartbeats quicken; which to dare?
One path leads to the well-known grind,
The other, mysteries entwined.

Branches arc, and shadows play,
In every choice, some heart may sway.
With every footfall, fate aligns,
As the night's silence softly chimes.

To choose is bold, to linger brave,
In the dark, our spirits save.
For every choice blooms fresh delight,
In paths diverging, life ignites.

Rewriting the Everyday Script

Each morning breaks with whispered dreams,
A canvas blank, where hope redeems.
We scribble lines in colors bright,
Turning shadows into light.

The mundane twists, a dance anew,
With every step, we find what's true.
Pages turn; we shape our fate,
In simple moments, love won't wait.

The coffee brews, a fragrant pause,
We celebrate the little flaws.
In laughter shared, our spirits lift,
A treasured tale, our greatest gift.

So here we stand, with ink in hand,
Crafting stories, bold and grand.
With courage fierce, we take our chance,
In rewriting life, we find our dance.

The Courage to Stray

In the stillness of the night,
A whisper calls, a flickering light.
A path less traveled beckons me,
To venture forth, to feel more free.

Each step away from comfort's hand,
Leads to wonders we had not planned.
With trembling heart, I dare to roam,
In every leap, I find my home.

The stars above, they guide my way,
Reminding me to seize the day.
In winding roads, adventure waits,
With every choice, we shape our fates.

So let me stray, let me explore,
Unlocking dreams I can't ignore.
For in the courage to depart,
I rediscover my true heart.

Invitations to the Unexpected

A knock at the door, who could it be?
Life's little gifts, wrapped playfully.
Moments surprise, like dancers' grace,
Filling the void, a warm embrace.

With open hands, I greet the chance,
To twirl through life's whimsical dance.
Every twist brings a brand new song,
In the unexpected, we all belong.

A phone call out of the blue,
A friend appears, a bond renewed.
In the smallest gestures, joy ignites,
Painting our days with brilliant lights.

So let us welcome what comes our way,
In laughter and love, we'll find our play.
With every heartbeat, let's take a stand,
Invitations bloom as life is planned.

Embracing the Unknown

Ahead lies a path, shrouded in mist,
A journey awaits, impossible to resist.
With every step, I shed my fear,
In the depths of silence, my heart is clear.

What lies beyond, I cannot see,
But in the unknown, I choose to be free.
Trusting the winds as they softly blow,
Guiding my spirit wherever to go.

Each dawn unveils a fresh delight,
The mysteries danced in morning light.
With courage as my trusty guide,
Through uncharted realms, I will glide.

So here I stand, embracing the change,
With open arms, I'll rearrange.
For in the unknown, life's wonders grow,
A rich tapestry, inviting me to flow.

Unmasking the Mundane

In the shadows, routines hide,
Whispers of color, dreams abide.
Each tick of clock, a chance to see,
Life's vibrant thread, wild and free.

Through tangled paths, we wander slow,
Finding beauty in the flow.
A stray leaf dances in the breeze,
Telling tales with graceful ease.

Moments flicker, like fireflies,
Revealing truths beneath our sighs.
In laughter's echo, wisdom waits,
Unmasking fate, the heart narrates.

Step by step, challenge the norm,
Burst the bubble, embrace the storm.
In the ordinary, magic glows,
As we learn, as our spirit grows.

A Symphony of Possibilities

Notes collide in vibrant thought,
Crescendo of dreams, never caught.
In silence, secrets come to play,
A melody of light, a brand new day.

Each brush of sound, a heartbeat shared,
In the chaos, we are prepared.
Harmonies soar, weaving through air,
A symphony built on hope and care.

Voices rise in tender refrain,
Echoes of joy, freedom from pain.
With every chord, we find our way,
A dance of life, in full array.

To weave our tales in vibrant hues,
Creating worlds with each insight we choose.
For in the music, we discover true,
Infinite paths, In me and you.

The Liberation of Intent

With every choice, the future bends,
A ripple of will, as time descends.
Intent ignites like morning's first light,
Setting free the dreams in flight.

Chains of doubt begin to break,
From stagnant pools, we rise awake.
Purpose forged in the quiet night,
Guiding hearts toward what feels right.

The journey's weight, both heavy and sweet,
In each heartbeat, possibilities greet.
With courage held in gentle hands,
We weave our fate through shifting sands.

As shadows fall, we embrace the thrill,
This liberation blooms at will.
In the tread of footsteps, life unfolds,
A tapestry of stories told.

Journey Beyond the Familiar

Step outside the comfort's thread,
Where the unknown is often dread.
Each breath a chance to redefine,
What it means to boldly shine.

With every turn, we seek the rare,
Uncharted paths, open and bare.
The compass spins, yet we remain,
Guided by desire, not by pain.

Mountains rise to greet our quest,
In every challenge, we are blessed.
Through valleys deep and skies so wide,
New horizons beckon; let's not hide.

The journey calls, a siren's song,
Inviting us to travel long.
For in the midst of all we find,
The spark of life, intertwined.

Rewriting My Story

With every turn of the page, I find,
A new refrain, a shift in mind.
The past, a whisper, fading away,
I step into light, embrace the day.

Old dreams linger, but new ones bloom,
In the garden of hope, I make room.
Words I once spoke, now fill me with fire,
I craft my path, let my soul inspire.

Each choice I make, a brushstroke bold,
Transforming the script that I once told.
In the chapters ahead, I see my truth,
A life reborn, reclaimed in youth.

In every line, my spirit soars high,
With courage and grace, I learn to fly.
This narrative's mine, penned with care,
A story renewed, a breath of fresh air.

When Comfort Becomes a Cage

Wrapped in the warmth of familiar days,
I wandered softly, caught in a haze.
The safe and the sound, a bittersweet tune,
Yet whispers of freedom hum like a rune.

The walls that embraced me now feel too tight,
As shadows of doubt encroach on my light.
I long to break free, to fearlessly roam,
To step out of safety and carve a new home.

Each breath that I take, a call to the wild,
The restless spirit, the dreamer, the child.
To dance with the storms and leap with the stars,
To shatter the silence and mend all the scars.

When comfort confines, it can swiftly stifle,
A cage made of love can dull the true rifle.
I stand on the edge, heart pounding anew,
To find my own wings and soar as I grew.

The Blossoming of Untamed Dreams

In the depths of the night, where visions ignite,
A tapestry woven with colors so bright.
The seeds of desire, planted with care,
As whispers of courage stir in the air.

Untamed and unbound, my heart knows the way,
To chase after stars at the break of the day.
With petals unfolding, I rise with the sun,
In the garden of dreams, my race has begun.

Every heartbeat a promise, a path to embrace,
The dance of the daring, in life's wildest chase.
With roots in the soil, I stretch to the sky,
The blossoming fervor, my spirit will fly.

As doubts cling like shadows, I will stand tall,
Embracing the chaos, I'll answer the call.
For the dreams within me are wild and profound,
A symphony of passion, in freedom I'm found.

Surrendering the Script

In the grip of the pen, I held tight the lines,
A narrative forged, with planned designs.
Yet life has a way of reshaping the stage,
As I turn the page, I let go of the rage.

To surrender the script, to trust in the flow,
With each breath, I learn to let go.
Imperfect and raw, I embrace what will be,
In the chaos of living, I finally see.

The character shifts, evolving with grace,
A journey uncharted, each step finds its place.
In the weave of existence, I find my own voice,
No longer a puppet, I make my own choice.

Releasing control, I dance with the wind,
In the fluidity, my heart starts to mend.
For in letting go, I discover the spark,
A story unwritten, igniting the dark.

Milton Keynes UK
Ingram Content Group UK Ltd.
UKHW032316121024
449481UK00011B/319